# THE POWER OF
# POSITIVE IMAGERY
## WITH THE
# LABYRINTH

BRENDEN HAUKOS

**BALBOA.**PRESS
A DIVISION OF HAY HOUSE

Balboa Press books may be ordered through booksellers or by contacting:

Balboa Press
A Division of Hay House
1663 Liberty Drive
Bloomington, IN 47403
www.balboapress.com
1 (877) 407-4847

Print information available on the last page.

ISBN: 978-1-9822-3683-0 (sc)
ISBN: 978-1-9822-3684-7 (e)

Balboa Press rev. date: 10/23/2019

This book is dedicated to the account
of the spirit of the planet.

# ONE

# GRATITUDE

You are a gift, of and unto the earth, the sun, and the sky, of your forebears, of the divinity, and of all things positive and present in this moment in time and in flux. You live in this moment. You live for this moment. Each day you work to slow the time, knowing that time moves forward unto the time you will pass on this gift, and the whisper of a river resonates in your heart.

Action committed with heart, to act with heart and walk a path with heart, these are all positive things. You embrace the positivity of all that is.

And even though there is potential for evil even in your own body, you are not afraid to face the evil in this world with an open mind and an open heart.

You are an ancient being – you are made of elemental things – and long ago you made a choice. Now you are resistant to evil. You resist evil, inside and out. And you know that the evils in this world are not meant to be understood. And it makes sense and it is positive that these things cannot be understood.

And even the pain of your own body – the pain is shot through with your body and your body is shot through with the pain. You and your pain are one. And even this is positive. Because pain is not evil. You are grateful, even for your pain.

And you are grateful for the darkness. You do not confuse the darkness for evil. You are a luminous being, and you walk a path of darkness and unknowing. This darkness and this unknowing is a tremendously positive thing.

You are a bearer of light. You cast shine and shadows everywhere you go. You are a bearer of earth, water, and fire also. You breathe the air, and the air also breathes you.

Boundless gratitude is a gift, and this gift belongs to you.

You cultivate images of gratitude, and these images nourish your body. You ask for images of positivity in all you think and do. You are happy.

Happiness is your inheritance, and it cannot be taken from you. You smile. You laugh. You cry. You are whole, yet you are also in flux.

You look into your thoughts, and you look underneath your thoughts, and you see a landscape of images, infinitely abounding. These images are in flux. And these images are shot through with your body. And your body is shot through with these images. You cultivate positive images, and these images nourish your body.

You look into one of these images. It passes before your eyes in slow motion. You see an image of the cycle of life. Of birth, growth, happiness, death, decay, rebirth. It is all in flux, and it is an image of positivity.

You watch a beet grow, you turn its fruit to juice, and you are nourished by the earth. The earth is your home. The earth and the ground, the silt and the soil. These are all tremendous and positive things.

You do not fear for the earth or for the damage that even you yourself have done to our habitat. You know that the earth will live out its life with or without us. And together we pray heartfully that the planet may live and die with grace.

As sad as it is to speak of the death of the planet, you know that even sadness is a positive thing. It is made up of images. And it is an elemental thing that makes up the images as it is made up of images. Gratitude is also an elemental thing.

You ask for images of boundless gratitude. You commit to being grateful for the beings in your life. You do not take these other beings for granted, as their bodies are also in flux. Their light casts shine and shadows on your heart. You walk together in darkness and unknowing, and together you are not afraid.

You seek gratitude, and you find it. When you meet yourself and others with boundless gratitude, you do the work of slowing time and living in this moment in time. You are grateful for each moment. You are an ancient being, and gratitude is part of your elemental make-up.

To you, ingratitude is as nothing. An element is not paired to its opposite, not in the world of positivity.

You cultivate images of boundless gratitude. And this nourishes your body.

You live in this moment of darkness and unknowing, and it is in this darkness and unknowing that is the place where we set the cornerstone. But no matter what structures we put up to shelter us from the sun and storm, we cannot shut out the darkness and unknowing.

You imagine gratitude as a bright white-purple light. Its radiant glow is beautiful, like the flicker of fireflies on a summer's eve. And you radiate beauty into the world when you close your eyes and imagine your body aglow with bright white-purple light. Your gratitude for the moment harmonizes the fluctuation of images and slows the passing of time.

Your mind is a wonderful thing, and full of surprises. You are filled with the light of boundless gratitude. It is possible to change the way you think in an instant. It is in this time that the time is right to fan the flames of gratitude and to take action. Sometimes sitting still is the act you will take to slow the spin of the great wide world.

Sitting still, you take time to remember your mother. You have one. Part of the story of this gift of life is the pain of mothers, of rearing and childbirth. Even if you have closed your heart to your mother, you commit now to ask for images of gratitude for all mothers, your mother among them.

You experience wonder in the face of the enormity of the universe. Wonder opens your heart and mind to the darkness and unknowing. Sometimes it all feels so good. And sometimes you run rampant with pain. You resolve to look the pain in the face, and in doing so, you allow the time to stretch out. This moment goes on and on.

Standing up, you take time to remember your father. You have one. Part of the story of this gift of life is the work that fathers do, attracting a mate, developing the growth and happiness of their children. Even if you have closed your heart to your father, you commit now to ask for images of gratitude for all fathers, your father among them.

Together we are unafraid. And you don't take any of it for granted.

At any point, you may have closed your heart to your mother or your father. As sad as it is, you may have closed your heart to many other people in this world. And, as painful as it is, other people may have closed their hearts to you. You remember that sadness and pain are also positive things, certain tunings of your body to the flux.

You ask now for an opening. You slowly open your heart, little by little, to all the beings who have come and gone in your life. You know that a healthy heart is an open heart. You are committed to the health of your heart and body. You renew your commitment in this very moment in time.

You recognize that gratitude, as an emotion, is a very healthy, healthful, and positive thing. Sadness is also healthy, healthful, and positive. You are grateful for the sadness you feel. It is a beautiful, painful, and very real and very positive thing. You are grateful for your sadness, and you are grateful for your gratitude, and you are grateful for the health you do have. And you don't take any of it for granted.

You sit a room with a dying man, and you hold his hand. In this moment you feel the sadness and pain of the passing of a dear friend as he hands on his torch. For this moment, this opportunity to say hi one last time, you are grateful. You are grateful for the humor you recognize still alive in your friend, even as he approaches death. You know that humor is healthy, and life is always full of bounteous health.

You return again and again to gratitude, bounteous gratitude, boundless gratitude. It all grows, little by little, through the flux of time. And in returning, you slow the time. And in not taking time for granted, you experience love for the time of your life. Sometimes it all feels so good.

The smile on your face, the smile in your heart – they are made of gratitude. As are the tears in your eyes. It is your strength that makes you cry. When you cry, you know that you are not done yet.

Maybe someday you shed a tear for the hatred you have held against other beings in your life, be they men or snakes. You are no longer afraid to share this world with men or snakes. With all life, great or small.

But you do not like all beings equally. You make a

commitment now to the little by little opening of your heart to the beings in your life that you do not like. This commitment uplifts you. You renew this commitment each day. Each day your heart opens wider. And the cooling waters of gratitude wash through your body.

Gratitude lives in the ground too. From seed a sunflower blooms up from the earth and faces the sun in gratitude for its loving light. It is a quiet and a positive thing when you lie on the earth and ask your body to absorb the gratitude from the grasses and the ground beneath you. Like the sun illuminating the images of the earth, gratitude illuminates the images in your mind and body.

You imagine gratitude as a bright white-purple light. You breathe in gratitude, and gratitude also breathes you in. This is a very positive, transformative process. You cultivate images of gratitude and boundless gratitude. These images are present in your body at this moment in time. And they change over time.

Your mind is brimming with positive imagery. You are not afraid to change, and you are not afraid to face the changes change will bring.

You are happy.

You are ever grateful.

TWO

# LOVE

Each day you renew your commitment to cultivate positive imagery. You cultivate images of gratitude, of boundless gratitude. You cultivate images of love, of undying love.

Love brings things together. To walk a path with heart, you know, is to follow the guidance of the heart at all turns, and your heart guides you with the light of love.

As fire, love is a burning desire, and it expires with the fade of a long night's embers. The cooling waters of love unite us in our separateness and hold us in their fluid embrace.

You imagine love as a bright rose light. You see your heart aglow in bright rose.

Lovers are bound together in love. They walk a path of knowing in the darkness.

You cultivate images of a circle of love, of the cycle of life. You seek these images, and seeking them you find them.

In this moment, for this moment, you are shot through with this moment, and this moment is shot through with you. You are a modern life-form. You are also an ancient being, made of elemental things. Love is the beating of your heart, in the knowing and the light, in the darkness of your chest. Love is the firmness of the ground beneath you.

Maybe you have been out on the ice in the cold and blowing, and drilling a hole through the crystal web of frozen lake, you cast your line into the depths, only to draw out a fish. And you are nourished by the earth. And there is love there, in solidarity with the harshness of elements.

The love of loves is an everlasting thing, bound together with the coming and going of elements in the swirls of forever. The love of loves is an unbroken link in the chain of the flux in the swirls of forever.

Your mind knows love. Your mind loves the truth. Hearing the truth, you take heed. In following a path with heart, you follow the gravity of truth down the path of knowing and light. The truth is that the positive imagery that you make up makes you up.

And love knows your mind. Love knows all things. Knowing evils, love rejects them. Love does not shine its light on evils. In the face of evil, love turns inward. This turning inward is the strength of love.

Darkness, however, is not evil. The darkness that obscures evil is a most necessary and positive thing.

"I will love you forever," you say to another, and it is true. Because love prevails over death. Death, which is a sad yet positive thing. Death, which is the transformation of a being into decay and unto rebirth.

Living now, you live forever in the light of the love of the divinity. The divinity loves love and all that love illuminates. You imagine love as a bright rose light, and it is beautiful to the divinity when you lie on your back on the earth and little by little breathe in love, and having breathed in love you radiate the light of love into the world of beings great and small. This is the work you do to slow the time. You show love and gratitude for the divinity as you do the work of slowing the time.

Work is the effort of love on a path with heart. Work bears its fruits. This fruit nourishes your body and the bodies of others. Your effort is a powerful and positive thing. Work illuminates the mind, body, and heart with the light of love.

In the world of separate forms, love is the love among an entity and its parts. Your toe loves your shoulder, and your shoulder loves it back. Love is the fiber that weaves together a whole being. This is love as earth, as all things solid and indivisible.

Love is endurant. Love endures pain. Your knee loves its pain, and pain loves it back. You listen for the truth of your pain, and hearing, you take heed.

You imagine yourself surfing the waves of the ocean of love, and this is an image of balance and skill and the spontaneous body, the body in play. There is love in work, and there is love in play. Your actions speak to the world, and the world responds. Sometimes it all feels so good. You are tickled by the world. You shiver.

You are made of blood, snot, saliva, and many other things. You cultivate images of health, happiness, and longevity. You drink water and taste its love for your body. Taking an ice cube, you feel its texture then its cold.

You are calm and relaxed. You radiate simple joy. You give happiness to others. These are the acts of love.

THREE

# THE CYCLE OF LIFE

Birth. Growth. Happiness. Death. Decay. Rebirth.
All stages of the cycle present in this moment.

Ancient beings. Modern beings. Being in the flux of time. Together and separate. Bonded by the stickiness of influence. The lives of animate and inanimate beings, stitched together by the friendships of matter.

You ask for images of the cycle of life. You ask for images of the swirls of forever. Your mind wants for knowledge, but it is imagery you seek. Images in excess of positivity.

You think the thought: "Happiness." Beneath this word, in your mind, is a foundation of images, infinitely abounding, in rows upon rows and columns upon columns. These images are not static – they transform over time. You nudge them toward positive transformation with the will of your mind and body.

Seeing the play of images and the cycle of life, you see how an eagle swims and a fish flies. They are bound together in the union of predator and prey, of eating and being eaten. The hunter runs with the deer – the deer waits with the hunter. They are bound together in a circle of love, the cycle of life.

It is not possible to speak of everything in purely positive terms. You do not dwell on the cruelty of, for instance, factory farming practices. Of course it is not enough to speak of a great love of chickens, pigs, cows, etc. for humans, though great that love may be. When confronted with phenomena such as this – and any phenomena at that – you adopt a stance of radical not-knowing. It is not that the truth is out there and your limited subjectivity cannot access it in itself. You recognize the truth as a uniquely human notion, and as far as you are human, the truth is as much inside of you as it is outside. The truth is, you know the stories, you see the images – the atrocity is very real, even unspeakable. You recognize that by retelling these stories and reproducing these images, you run the risk of vitalizing something that might best be left to rot. At the same time you know that what you know to be an atrocity truly is an atrocity, but the truth is primordially and inextricably bound up in perceptual, political, communicative, lingual, narrative, historical, etc. contingencies. The foundation of not-knowing is this –you do not know what you are. You do not know what you do, what should be done, if anything, or what it is that happens when you do do something. What is it that truly happens at the site of factory farms? Not-knowing, you cannot ask the question.

You do not, however, use not-knowing as justification for wrong- or evil-doing. Quite the opposite. In the spirit of not-knowing, you make the only possible choice – happiness, via the cultivation of positive images. You do this not knowing whether the choice is a free one.

The world of positivity is a place within and among shadows and darkness. Your life is almost undoubtedly bound up in patterns of consumption and movement and being that are in turn bound up with acts of cruelty and evil. If this means your life is cast entire into darkness, then you put your hands up and accept that even that is a positive thing. You choose to walk a path with heart, despite the conundrum you face.

You cultivate images of flourishing in the winds of uncertainty. Your mind does not have all the answers. Sometimes you throw your hands up and say, "Why? Why?

Why? Why? Why? Why me? Why was I even born?" This is the moment of despair.

You are brought to the question of agency. What choices have I ever had in all of this? And in the face of death, what choice do I have anyway? The world is full of violence, agents of violence and acts of violence. You are tempted to hang your head. In fact, you have fallen face-first in the murk a few times already in this life, and in this life you have almost drowned in that same murk before rising up, covered in sludge, the image of dejected monstrosity.

You wash yourself clean in the waters of life. You turn away from evil, and in doing so, you choose something greater than ignorance. You do not acknowledge him whose voice you would not hear. You choose a path of positivity in a realm where light shines on all things, and evil appears naked before your very eyes. You are not afraid to face the evil of this realm with an open mind and an open heart.

You remember that the evils that exist in this world are not meant to be understood. You have images of evil in your body. You ask for a cessation of these images.

You imagine life as a bright green light. You cultivate positive images of the cycle of life, and your images of this cycle are shot through with the color green.

You see happiness in life, and you remember happiness is your inheritance. No one can take it from you.

You can change the way you think in an instant.

The earth is literally on fire with the burning of petrol. Who will be the one to flood the earth with the cooling waters of love? And what will rise from the ashes? What will arise from the decay of all the chemical compounds and splitting of atoms? The story of the earth is told a thousand times, a thousand thousand times. Yet the future remains uncertain, unseen.

Where will your body go when you die? And what will rise from your ashes? Will you return to the earth? Will you one day be shot through with earthworms? It is hard to smile when your face is stuck in the murk.

You do the work of slowing the time, of appreciating the comings and goings of things inside and outside your body, and slowly you learn to smile. The coming and going of things is the cycle of life.

You do not despair. The divinity is always near. You live with the divinity in the swirls of forever.

And you are ever alive, alight with the bright green element of life, in the cycles of life.

FOUR

# SADNESS

S adness is a small thing. It comes little by little. It comes and goes with the coming and going of things. You see sadness in a positive light.

You imagine sadness as a bright light-blue light. In your time of need, you lie on your back, close your eyes, and imagine your body surrounded and filled with the bright light-blue light of sadness. This light is a comfort to you in your time of grief and loss.

You feel sadness, and you do not try to hold onto it, nor do you try to make it go away. You feel its fullness, its emptiness, and its transience.

You see sadness in yourself. You see yourself in sadness. You imagine sadness as an image of day passing into night, the bright blue twilight. It is all so good, even when it feels bad. Sadness does not always feel good. Very rarely does it.

You cultivate images of the cycle of life, and in doing so, you cultivate images of sadness. You do not mistake sadness for evil. Evil is not a positive thing. It is cast into darkness. Sadness is a tuning of the body to the changing times and to evil. Sadness does not shine its light on evil. This is the mystery of darkness.

You do not dwell on the evil of evils. Is the man who commits one evil cast into darkness entire? Is evil an eternal matter? You do not dwell on these questions.

You make your dwelling in the world of positivity. The element of darkness casts evil into non-being. Evil does not participate in all that is, not in the world of positivity. Your heart draws a bending line in the swirls of forever.

What constitutes evil? You let the question come, and you let it go. The thought of evil saddens you.

You do not seek out sadness. When the time is right,

sadness will seek you out. It will come, and it will go. It will be forever insinuated in the elemental make-up of your being, a great sadness, a bright blue glimmering light, the heart of matter's heart.

The turning away of matter from its parts, from the evil in its body, is a tremendous and sad and tremendously sad and positive thing. You remember that evil cannot be understood, and this saddens you, and it uplifts you.

You commit each day to the cultivation of heart in your life, and you are nourished by the earth.

FIVE

# ANGER

Y ou are full of blood, bile, spit and all the rest. There is no escape from anger and the unprettier things.

The world is a vile place. The evil that makes up some of the fiber of your being can sicken you to the marrow of your bones. You could scream, if only you didn't hold yourself back. Anger sputters in spittle from the rasps of your lips. Nothing is good. Nothing will ever be okay. Your dreams will never come true. All of it unmatters equally.

You'd like to tear someone's head off. The littlest slight swells into the enormity of volcanic insult. Deep breaths don't quell the burning. You fight back hot tears. What can you say? What can you do? What can you even feel? You say to yourself, "Fuck this fucking shit, and fuck this fucking shit."

What is life if not a miserable display of impotent power? An endless series of disappointments? A powerless keening of those who want hopelessly for nothing but not to die?

There is no accounting for what lies in the depths of your heart and mind. Your anger goes beyond comprehension. The images in your mind are beyond the will you have for them. You have relinquished control into the hands of all that is terrible and tormenting in your body.

Stop.

You stop yourself. Without hope for the future, you can harbor no regrets.

It is not that what you feel is untrue. The emphasis of truth, the truth of truths, and the ultimately true – you can see this now as uniquely, and unhelpfully, human.

You cultivate images of anger as a positive thing, a tempering force eliminating impurities.

You imagine anger as a bright black light. It is part of the elemental make-up of your being. And a great teacher.

You ask now for a cessation of anger in your mind and body.

# SIX

# THE CHAINS OF BONDAGE

When you look to the past, at the events of your life, times lived out, you may see cycles of behavior that have ruled over you, led you astray. It's as if you have gone so far and can tread no farther. The chains of bondage – be they attitudes, concepts, relationships, habits, addictions, desires, identifications, or mere notions – they have set the limits of your life for you.

It is in this time of self-recognition that the time is right to stage a coup. You will resume leadership of your own life. You enact this via the cultivation of positive images. You cultivate images of redirection, reversal, and renewal, images of overcoming adversity, images of replacing unwanted habits with wanted ones. You seek these images, and seeking them, you find them. Through this dedicated process, you slowly but inexorably sunder the chains of bondage.

You say goodbye to attitudes that diminish you. Though they may appear to be truths, negative attitudes are in truth anathema to life. You create images of yourself as a person who embraces a positive attitude. You refuse to give up. And you refuse to give in to the allure of negativity.

You recognize the chains of bondage even when they masquerade as the reality principle. You eschew notions of optimism, pessimism, and realism for positive imagery that is not simplistic or naïve but favorably complex.

You say goodbye to concepts that lead to bondage. Instead, you embrace a mindful openness to your experiences and perceptions. You commit to stay raw. You find positive images inside and outside of you, and you let this imagery remain raw. Images resist conceptualization, you see, and seeing this, you see that images will not bind you in chains.

Your choice to cultivate positive images is an affirmation of life, happiness, and health.

You say goodbye to the people, though they may call themselves friends, who would rather see you pinned to the earth than elevated. You recognize these people as foes, but you do not confront them. You merely turn your back. You are alone, at one. You create images of distance between yourself and your foes. This distance is full of the abyss, and it is impassable.

You say goodbye to habits that are no longer wanted. You cultivate images of replacing these unwanted habits with wanted ones. Instead of smoking cigarettes, you drink water, eat clean foods, and exert yourself in exercise. You refrain from telling yourself that what you are doing is not easy. You cultivate images of yourself rising to meet challenges, facing them fearlessly. You live with measured abandon.

You recognize unwanted habits that call out to you from the shadows of every room and each new situation. These are addictions. You remember that addiction is not something that afflicts you – it is something that you do. Stop doing it, and you are no longer addicted.

You say goodbye to your addiction, once and for all. And its defeat is the little by little momentum that results in your liberation.

You say goodbye to those desires that have led you astray. Desire is a primal force, an ancient element. It drives you from the inside out, and from the outside in. For as long as you remember, your desire has been with you, in you. It burns a hot, bright red. You imagine desire burning in the core of your body. You close your eyes and feel its heat and its pulse. You cultivate images of yourself honing the focus of your desire and channeling it in the direction of your hopes and dreams. This process nourishes your will and gives it strength. You begin anew, without rejecting your past or judging its worth.

You say goodbye to the identifications that bind you to ways you desire to leave behind. You identify with yourself and nothing else. You slip loose from the frigid rigidity of language. You see your actions as raw postures, the willful transition points between the past and the future. You do not, however, see your actions as stitching points to any identity that exists outside of time or the body. This is a method for using your thoughts to liberate yourself, as opposed to letting your thoughts weigh you down.

You say goodbye to the self that allows mere notions to guide you through your days. You cultivate images of living deliberately, yet always with measured abandon. Notions are like the winds that try and sometimes succeed to alter your direction as you traverse the landscape of living. You may delight in its cooling touch on a hot day, or at the times when it is at your back, pushing you in the direction of your aims and dreams. But when the winds ride full force against you, stealing all momentum, you put your head down and bear down against it, unceasing in your purpose.

You have unlocked the cuffs of the chains of bondage, and while their iron grasp has chafed the skin of your neck, wrists, and ankles, you know that time will heal those wounds too. You are free, here and now, and while this is an arrival, it is also just the beginning.

SEVEN

# DIFFERENCES

Things come, and things go. You seek positive images of the flux of time and the vast expanses of differences. You are grateful for the other beings in your life, and in your gratitude, you do not define other beings. You do not wish to see them bound in the chains of your making. In awe of mystery, you do not distinguish even between living and non-living. You do not see yourself as an arbiter of ultimate meaning.

You try to distinguish between what is inside of you and what is outside of you. Looking out, you see that you are also outside of yourself. Looking out, you see also that what is not you is inside of you.

You do not identify as human, nor do you proclaim a universal, scientific conception of humanity. You recognize that a term that includes, like humanity, always already excludes. And again, you do not consider yourself an arbiter of such things. Looking out, you see the vast expanses of differences, and looking in you see the same.

Differences are dissolved in interrelation. At the same time, differences are concretized in struggle. There is no ultimate truth here. Without light, there is no reflection.

Your experience of self is earth, and it is water. It is of a concrete self ground against outside matters, a definite centrality that utters "I..." It is also a fluid consciousness that shares consciousness with all consciousness, an I that does not utter "I..." and exists outside of yourself but not in any centralized location – an unspeakable being being being.

There are differences, then, within yourself.

You do not dwell forever on the confusion these matters engender. You relax into an openness to the mystery of your experience. You don't do the act of identifying. You like to think of yourself as like a gardener, planting the seeds of positive imagery.

You witness the play of images, inside and outside of yourself. You share this imagery with all other beings, with being itself.

The vast expanses of differences are shot through with the images you cultivate. Your heart draws a bending line in the swirls of forever, and each line is different, each luminous heart a singularity.

Love entwines two hearts and eradicates all distance between but not any differences between two things. You cultivate images of love as a passionate exchange of differences.

On a mundane level, you cultivate images of respect for differences, in yourself and in other beings. You respect your own way of life, and through that, you can respect different ways of life. The distance between these is necessary for differences to arise.

You let things come, and you let things go. You give them their distance, and the violence that you can avoid you do avoid. You cultivate images of nonviolent responses to different situations. And you pray heartfully for a cessation of violence amidst the flourishing of differences.

EIGHT

# TRANQUILITY

All things calm and bright. At home. In motion. Fluctuating tides. Flickering surfaces. Everything together as one. In communion with itself. Forever and ever. Being beyond belief. Events great and small. Unto the infinite. Abounding. In the knowing and the light. The choice already made, reflected forever in your heart and in mine. With endless distance between us. Vastness beyond vastness. Forever beyond change. Swirling. In an everlasting stillness. In consort with the elements. Radiant through and through. Alight. And colorful. A harmonization of parts. The cooling flow of waters. The tenderness of grass. Soft earth. Firm earth. The breathing in. The breathing out. All things. Calm and bright. Breathed in. And out. For the duration. Endurant. Bodies and breaths. The heartbeat. Of animate and inanimate beings. The friendships of matter. Images upon images. Unto the infinite. Aspected to interrelation. All perspectives at all times. And all combinations of things. And all possibilities cycling side by side in everlasting variation. And you. Alone. At one. Among. All things. Calm. And bright.

# THE LABYRINTH

S omeone has been stepping in the murk. The waters of your mind are turbid and permit nothing to be seen. It is you – you who have been tramping through puddles on the dirt paths within the labyrinth.

Are you confused?

I know that I am. Deeply confused. Dare I say profoundly confused? – here in this place.

This place – the labyrinth – it is inside of you and it is outside of you – it is real and it is imagined. It is inescapable, although you are not actually even here. Within the depth of this place, the Minotaur waits and grows hungry – he is you, and he is not you.

"Escape!" you say. "We must escape this place. All I want in the world is to get out of here. As far back as I can remember, that's all I ever wanted."

We can't remember much, you and I.

"If you actually knew what you truly wanted, and then you got it for yourself, might it not still feel empty?" I say.

"All I want is to get out of here. I can worry about the rest later," you say.

You are tired and weary. Tired from fighting against yourself. Weary from fighting with me. We have been lost here together, walking one hall after another, and our feuds have been bitter and cruel. We set out long ago – how long ago neither of us can remember – in search of nature, in search of our natures, and where we came to is lost and trapped and caught in the trap of our loss in the illusion of reality and the reality of illusion.

I am here to tell you, there is a way. You must first have a vision. You must first see, and then you may go. And where we're going, you must learn to see in the dark. You must pass through the crucible that is the Minotaur.

Beware. Beware of fear. Beware the fear of the Minotaur. As I've said, the Minotaur is a crucible you must pass through. Your body, too, is a crucible – it is the fiery place where experience experiences itself.

To speak of the need for a vision is not to say that you can just wish to see yourself outside of here. In a world that is inside-out, even the outside is in. I cannot describe to you the details, nor perhaps do they particularly matter outside of their own time and place, but in other cultures young people were guided to leave society for a time on their own in search of a vision. In our own society, there is no such initiation into meaning and maturity. Our only initiation is into a life of indebtedness or at the very least servitude. We are all forever children, ambling the halls of the labyrinth.

You tell me that I am as lost as you are, and that I shouldn't be lecturing you. I tell you that this is about you, not me, and to turn things back on a person like that is a childish form of argumentation. But the subtlety of my point of view is either lost on you, or it is a delusion of mine.

"It was all a mistake," you say, "setting out in search of a better life."

"It was entering this labyrinth that was our mistake," I say.

"Why did we come here?" you ask.

"I don't know," I say.

"Did we have a choice?" you ask.

"I cannot remember," I say. Maybe that was our mistake all along. We've somehow forgotten everything we need to know.

If only we could remember…

If only…

"If only we could understand balance…" I say.

"As if that would help us out of here," you say.

"You and I don't exactly see eye to eye, do we?" I ask.

"What was your first clue?" you ask.

"What I'm saying is, if we can't find happiness here together, how can we ever expect to find it outside of here?" I ask.

"Because out there, that's freedom," you say.

"Right now, I'm not even convinced there is an 'out there' out there," I say.

"And what could you possibly mean by that?" you ask.

"What I mean is, maybe this labyrinth wasn't created to hold us in. Maybe the labyrinth created us."

"Oh the labyrinth gave birth to me, did it?' you ask.

"Precisely," I say.

"And who are you, my fucking father?" you ask.

"Far from it," I say.

"I'm sick of this nonsense," you say. "What were you saying about balance anyway?"

I sigh, then look up to the heavens, speckles of light playing spiral patterns across my vision.

We walk in silence for a time.

"It is my belief," I say, "that the world is in balance. When I say the world, I mean everything that is. The world is in balance, though it may not appear so to us. I would even argue that the apparent lack of balance we perceive is in fact a balancing of the balance that reigns true in the world, part of the balancing act that is the world we live in," I say.

"Hmm," you say. "But what exactly is balance? How do you define it?"

"Balance is a serpent, slithering sinuously. It is the Wanderer, or perhaps Wanderings," I say.

"In other words, you don't know," you say.

"Precisely. But I will say this: a person often assumes, about balance, that things are balanced by their opposites, and often time is factored into the equation. For example, a certain length of time spent in one state, say sadness, is balanced by an equal length of time spent in the opposite state, say joy. I don't really hold this assumption to be true, at least not necessarily so. Think of a scale, where something is balanced by something of equal weight. And maybe intensity is the measure of things. I don't know why the thought occurs to me, but think of sadness and joy — maybe they are opposites due to their matching respective intensities, and the fact that one is considered positive and the other negative," I say.

"I don't know," you say.

"And I don't know either," I say.

Over time the sky begins to tremble and then to swell into a heavenly blue. When the blue has faded into black, we know the night is upon us. We continue on, without tiring, for in the labyrinth our bodies are not as we'd expect them to be.

"Do you mind," you say. "I'd like to stop for now. For all we know we're only retracing our steps."

I know you're right in this, though for all my philosophizing I'm still impatient for a sense of progress, desperate for the next breakthrough.

You lie on a dry patch and gaze at the stars, inventing

your own constellations, while I sit cross-legged and look to the backs of my eyelids, trying to maintain a calm state of focus and clarity of mind.

Maybe an hour has passed, maybe three. "For the first time in my life, I have seen the stars," you say. "And boy have they travelled a long way to see me."

And then, later, you ask, "When you said we have to learn to see in the dark, what did you mean?"

"To see in the dark," I say, eventually, "is to see beyond the veil of mundane reality and everyday decision-making into the deeper darkness of the way of choices becoming and bringing about the future. The past, well, the past lives in the present as the memory of how the future will be. We must see beyond the specter of the past. Our eyes must penetrate the unknown. In other words, we must see in the dark. We must foresee."

And later yet, I say, "I have had a vision – a vision of a way out of here."

"We must learn to fly," you say.

"We must learn," I concur, "to fly."

"But first…" you start.

"First we must slay the Minotaur," I finish.

"We are going to slay the Minotaur, who may be hunting us as we speak," you say.

"He does not hunt but await us. He knows deeply the power of fear that draws us into his ever-tightening circle. He knows that in our need we will need to face him. And his own fear of destruction fuels his consuming power."

"How is it," you ask, "you know the Minotaur so well?"

Memories have been flooding back into me, and as you

look at me with the heat of the question in your eyes, I feel a twinge of fear somewhere in my midsection.

"I hesitate to answer," I say.

"My suspicion is already beyond burgeoning, so speak the truth, old man," you say.

"He is my son," I say.

"I am not surprised," you say.

"You are angry," I say.

"I'm not angry," you say. "The spell you have me under slowly deteriorates. But I am not so stupid as to think I won't need your help in escaping this place."

"I was put under the same spell, Theseus," I say.

"Hush. No more of that," you say.

"I..."

"Who created the labyrinth?" you ask.

"A great inventor and architect," I say. "The greatest. Daedalus. He was able to create this place to house the monster that stems from my own wayward seed. He created it in the physical realm and in the realm of the mind, all of our minds. Such was his prowess, such his gift. And he did this at such a cost. I repaid his debt by feeding the pathetic man – oh how pathetic they all are in the face of such horror, oh how indignant their tongue at the taste of such vile betrayal – I fed him to the Minotaur and thus sealed this place with his sacrifice. Here in this place, beyond a peculiar switchback in the recesses of our minds, the Minotaur holds sway – but beyond that, out there...OUT THERE...he is as nothing. You must see that I did as I must?"

"A sordid tale."

"The frayed seams of responsibility's heavy garment."

"Keep talking, old man. As you spew your fancy words, we both grow old. But Daedalus is dead."

But in that moment, I do not keep talking. With a sharp intake of breath, I stop where I am and stare.

"What is it?" you ask.

I point, and your eyes follow the line of my vision down to a crack at the base of the labyrinth's wall. A sparkling gold filament creeping out of it.

"A golden thread!" I exclaim.

"What is it?" you repeat.

"It is our path…" I say.

"The way out…" you say.

"…our path to the Minotaur," I say.

And you say nothing.

"Close your eyes," I say.

"I will not…" you are saying.

"Do as I've told you!" I say.

Your eyes meet mine in a moment of aggravated defiance, but after a second you close them.

"We must become small. To face the Minotaur, we must become small like him," I say. "Now, keep your eyes closed, and focus on your breath. With every in-breath, breathe in strength. Feel the strength of the world as it stitches together the fibers of your being. Now breathe out, and as you breathe out, imagine yourself getting smaller and smaller. Do this again and again until you are the size of an ant."

I go silent. The sound of our breathing is all there is, as time fluctuates around our bodies in a great kaleidoscopic flurry.

I fall to one knee and, scraping my fingers across the dirt, feel the closeness of the ground. "Open your eyes."

I look at you, and I recognize the wonder within your

gaze as it ascends to the glimmering image of a golden rope before us trailing off into the darkness beyond a large, moldering portal. Above the portal, the walls of the labyrinth loom large as mountains buried in the sea.

"With the help of this golden thread, we really can see in the dark," I say.

We lock eyes, and after a second, you say, "From here forward, no more talk." And your blade is drawn.

You lead the way along the trail of the golden thread. With each footfall, each muted breath, each rustle of cloth, I try to measure the weight of your fear. To my surprise, I sense only calm purpose and a relaxed intensity of focus. A true warrior you are, O Theseus. And your solid core of courage strikes fear in my own heart.

Time passes, and we travel deeper into the maw of the labyrinth.

You stop, frequently, trying to sense his presence. As I have said, the Minotaur waits and grows hungry. There will be no ambush.

The truth of this becomes apparent. We hear him before he hears us. We come to a clearing, and against the far wall, we see the Minotaur standing. His brown horns gleaming in the moonlight. His eyes transfixed on an indistinct point before him. His voice growing ever louder.

We listen, as he utters his fell incantation: "Fear of death. Fear of the unknown. Fear of what the future will bring. Fear of rejection. Fear of failure. Fear of change. Fear that things will stay the same. Fear of Hell. Fear of God. Fear of pain and suffering. Fear of disease. Fear of spiders. Fear of exposure. Fear of being alone. Fear of heights. Fear of losing. Fear of losing control. Fear of wasting your life. Fear of being maimed. Fear of apocalypse. Fear of being stupid. Fear of being misunderstood. Fear of enclosed spaces. Fear of public speaking. Fear of drowning. Fear of burning. Fear of being less than someone else. Fear of being ugly or unattractive. Fear of being on top. Fear of having no food or clean water. Fear of betrayal. Fear of the dark. Fear of monsters. Fear of natural catastrophe. Fear of destitution. Fear of abandonment. Fear of losing loved ones. Fear of authority. Fear of anarchy. Fear of suicide. Fear of everyday things going awry..."

"Quiet!" you yell, leaping forward into a battle stance. "The time for fear is past, Minotaur. Death approaches."

The Minotaur charges. You wait, then feint left, then actually go left. Your blade arcs down. The Minotaur's head rolls in the dust.

In my astonishment at the beauty of your killing blow, I almost don't take a moment to see the rotting poetry of my own gesture. You turn, and seeing everything forever too late, you barely flinch as I slip my dagger underneath your ribs and up into your beating heart.

"My king..." you say, with your last words.

And the thought trailed off. King Minos looked up from the banquet table at the faces seated around it, all watching him with rapt attention. The memory of all that had happened within the labyrinth slunk away like a miserable servant. He cleared his throat to finish his tale.

"And with the last of his strength, Theseus held fast to the Minotaur's wrist as it pressed the dagger into his chest. And with his dying breath, he let out a piercing cry. And in his final act as a mortal man, Theseus brought down his own blade and chopped the Minotaur's head to the ground. A great hero has fallen."

King Minos held up his chalice.

"Tonight we remember the slayer of monsters. Tonight we remember the savior of the realm. Tonight we remember the final victim of the Minotaur. Tonight we remember Theseus. A nobler and dearer man I have never known. To Theseus!"

"To Theseus!"

And he drank deep.

Printed in the United States
By Bookmasters